All pieces in this collection are original. The Sappho fragment in *The Encounter with Sappho* is quoted directly from *The Pocket Sappho*, translated by Willis Barnstone (p. 41).

First Edition
ISBN: 978-1-0673529-0-5
Printed in Canada

UNBECOMING

Poems, Prose, Letters, and Echoes

Natália Vaněčková

For Martina —
the everlight that kept me from the shadows,
the pulse that carried me through the dark,
and the reason I am here today.

Table of Contents

Introduction: The Quiet Unfolding

I. Origins

I have always loved language, not just for the way it speaks, but for the way it listens. As a child, I filled notebooks with scattered lines or simple fragments. They were an attempt to hold onto something fleeting: a sound, a thought, a feeling too large for conversation. I didn't have the words yet, not in English and not quite in Slovak or Czech either. I was an ESL student, suspended between multiple tongues, learning that language itself could be its own form of migration.

When I began studying English literature, it was as though a door I had been pressing my ear against finally opened. I devoured everything I could find: Voltaire's satire, Shelley's trembling light, Byron's melancholy, the quiet ache of John Donne. I inhaled Wilde's wit, Stoker's shadows, and, above it all, Tolkien's imagined worlds that often felt truer than reality. Later, through the *Norton Anthology of English Literature*, I walked through entire centuries, guided by voices that refused to fade.

During my first year at university, I wrote an essay comparing my own creative process with that of the acclaimed composer Hans Zimmer. I still remember the title, *Connecting Arts: A Comparison of a Personal Creative Process to Hans Zimmer's Film Scoring Method*. I was all about engaging the senses and finding a way to give life to what was stirring within me. When my professor returned it, she wrote at the bottom of the paper, alongside my grade of A: *"Natalia, the content here is highly engaging, interesting, and relevant. Exceptionally readable and excellent."*

As an ESL student, receiving that note of encouragement gave me the push I needed to believe that perhaps I was on the right path, especially after professors who dismissed my work, telling me I should "go back to fifth grade" or questioning why I was even there, suggesting I "go back to Russia." Mind you, I am not Russian, but Czech and Slovak, and having my heritage so carelessly misidentified made the remark cut deeper – a reminder that my identity, like my voice, could be dismissed or misunderstood. In short, that single encouraging note from the creative writing professor reminded me that my effort, perspective, and existence as a writer mattered.

And yet, it was not only the English canon that formed me. I found myself drawn to the precision of Ibsen, the serenity of Bashō, and, more recently, the layered melancholy of Joseon-era tales by the incredible June Hur, which reminded me of how I felt walking through the old palaces in Seoul, South Korea, for the first time in 2010. Each of these voices revealed a different rhythm of truth, showing how the same emotion could take on countless shapes depending on culture, time, and silence. But it was Sappho who changed everything.

II. The Encounter with Sappho

The first time I heard the name Sappho was when I was quite young. One of our very first family vacations, in 1997, took us to Greece. We spent a solid month exploring the area around Nei Pori, including a trip to Mount Olympus, and visits to the Archaeological Park of Dion and Platamon Castle. Even though I learned that Sappho had been a poet of ancient times, I was far more interested in the myths of Ancient Greece and splashing around in the Aegean Sea.

So, Sappho, the woman whose name was always spoken in reverence, always bracketed by words like "lyric" and "fragment" remained an echo I could not quite reach for years. It was not until a women's writing class at university that I truly met her on the page. Her surviving lines trembled with intimacy and power, as if they had been waiting across centuries for someone to listen. And then came Eros:

"Love shook my heart like wind on a mountain punishing oak trees."[1]

That line took my breath away. Not for its beauty—though it is undeniably beautiful—but for its recognition. For the first time, I saw in poetry the same quiet ferocity I had felt in life. It was not ornate. It was not guarded. It was raw, unashamed, and completely human.

In that moment, Sappho became more than a poet. She became permission. Permission to feel without apology, to let tenderness and strength coexist in the same breath, to write without softening the truth. That single encounter changed the way I saw writing forever.

III. The Next Steps

I have always loved language for the worlds it opens and the doors it quietly closes. Perhaps that is why I have never been content with knowing just one. Wherever I went, I made it a point to learn, to listen, even to the smallest words. "When in Rome, do as the Romans do" is not simply etiquette; it is reverence.

---

[1] Quoted directly from *The Pocket Sappho*, translated by Willis Barnstone (p. 41).

I learned phrases in the languages of the places that shaped me. I studied Japanese long enough to earn my JLPT N4[2]. I dabbled in French, Danish, Italian, Greek, and Korean — each a window into another way of breathing. Some of it I have forgotten, as all neglected languages fade. But I know that if I were to return, the words would remember me.

There has always been a strange magic in language, the way it rebuilds you through listening. It reminds me that identity is not static; it is multilingual, ever-shifting, like the tide.

I started writing my own fragments as a young teen, trying to create awkward rhymes with moon, bloom, gloom. They were clumsy, sentimental, sometimes unbearably earnest. But they were mine. At first, I did not share them. One of the very first test readers was my best friend Tsarina, who would intently read anything I managed to craft nearly every morning before school. I would watch her closely, waiting for her reaction: "Is it any good?" She always encouraged me to keep going, because she was entertained. In a way, she has a hand in the fact that I am a writer today. Without her, I probably would not have continued writing so diligently.

Later, my dear friend Natasha would offer the same kind of encouragement. She never cared what I wrote; her advice was simple: "Just write. Word vomit, then edit later. It is fine." With her encouragement, I dove into fan fiction writing during my university studies. It was easier to create something from established characters and explore plot, which gave me the freedom to experiment while still keeping up with academic writing. This dual

---

[2] *JLPT N4 refers to the fourth level of the Japanese Language Proficiency Test, demonstrating the ability to understand basic Japanese used in everyday situations, including simple reading and writing.*

practice allowed me to sharpen my analytical skills for essays while keeping my creative voice alive. Anytime I shared something with her, she cheered me on and read it with genuine interest.

This is why, as a fiction writer, I fully support fan fiction. It is a vibrant form of storytelling that fosters creativity, community, and engagement. Besides, many works we now call classics are really a form of fan fiction. Dante's *La Divina Commedia* draws on older myths and epics, Milton's *Paradise Lost* retells Genesis, and Shakespeare's most famous play, *Hamlet*, adapts the centuries-old Norse tale of Amleth.

Through fan fiction, I discovered that stories can connect us across languages, cultures, and decades. Messages from readers around the globe – some in French, Portuguese, Japanese, English, or Spanish – became part of the encouragement that shaped me as a writer. Even if the words are not always remembered in full, the sense that someone out there is reading, responding, and imagining alongside you is a powerful gift. It taught me that writing is never a solitary act. It is a conversation across time and space, a shared imagination that binds creators and readers together. Every story is part of a larger tapestry, woven from countless voices and perspectives. It reminded that creativity thrives in community, that ideas evolve as they are reshaped, and that the connections forged through stories – empathy, reflection, shared excitement – are as meaningful as the stories themselves.

IV. The Shape of Unbecoming

I never intended to publish this collection. For years, these pieces lived quietly in notebooks, tucked between drafts of stories and the chapters of worlds I was building elsewhere. They were fragments written in the margins of my life, never meant to stand together. By nature, I am a fiction writer. I gravitate toward world-building, toward layered mysteries and expansive narratives that unfold slowly, chapter by chapter. Storytelling, for me, has often meant invention. Perhaps one day soon, I will publish my first novel, inspired deeply by my roots. But this collection is something a beautiful start.

Unbecoming began as a quiet act of returning to myself. It is not a neat narrative, nor a sequence of beginnings and endings. Rather, it is a series of thresholds. Each piece is a fragment, a meditation, a travelogue of emotion and memory.

To "unbecome" is not to erase yourself. It is to peel back the names, stories, and expectations that were never truly yours. It is to look at what remains, the raw pulse beneath it all, and recognize it as enough.

These writings are not only about love, grief, or transformation. They explore movement across places, time, and selves. They trace the journey of becoming through the simultaneous act of undoing, shedding, remembering, forgiving, and reimagining.

When I wrote them, I didn't intend to capture a timeline. Instead, I found myself writing echoes. The writings began speaking to one another across oceans, across decades, across lives. They blurred geography and memory until the difference no longer mattered.

V. To My Sister

And at the center of all of it, the reason this book exists is my sister. When I was twelve, the world felt unbearably heavy. I almost did not make it across that bridge. But she was there. She stood like a fortress when everything else fell away. She became the reason I learned to breathe again. This collection is, at its deepest, a love letter — to survival, to those who hold us when we cannot hold ourselves.

Martina, this book, and the life it represents, is because of you.

You are my Everlight.

Coda: The Quiet Offering

With all that I have said, I offer these writings not as answers, but as mirrors. They are small reflections of the countless selves I have become and unbecome, the quiet lives lived between languages, silences, and breaths. Each writing began as a whisper, a single thread pulled from memory or dream. Some were written in moments of clarity, others in the half-light of forgetting. Together, they form a map — not to a destination, but circling back endlessly to the act of being human.

If these words reach you, I hope they do so gently. I hope they remind you that there is grace in imperfection, courage in continuing, and that unbecoming is not a loss, but a return.

To live, after all, is to rewrite ourselves constantly — to choose presence over disappearance, tenderness over silence. To live is to listen.

And if, in some small way, these writings help you listen — to yourself, to others, to the world as it trembles quietly beneath its own weight—then every word was worth it.

—Natália

PART I. Becoming

The emergence of self, through memory, place, language, and reflection — a gentle unfolding

Becoming

I have shed so many names to find the one that fits
Each version of me left a whisper behind –
A girl who dreamed,
A woman who dared to stay.

Becoming is no thunderclap
But the soft unfurling of truth,
A slow return to the pulse,
Beneath the noise.

I am not who I was,
Nor yet who I will be –
Somewhere in between,
I am finally home.

Wildflower, part I

I bloom where none believe I could,
Through stone, through storm,
Misunderstood.
No gardener's hand, no careful plan,
Through it all, I stand.

Not prized, perhaps,
Nor neatly grown,
But I have made the sun my own.
A little wild, a little stray,
I rise, I flourish, come what may.

Where the Rivers Meet

I carry two names upon my tongue,
The soft cadence of valleys,
The quiet of rolling hills.
Each one sings of rivers that once ran together,
Of forests that held our ancestors' laughter,
Of markets and kitchens where life was kneaded
Into bread and stories.

Borders may mark the land,
But they cannot still the pulse beneath my skin.
I am both the wind over the Tatras,
And the mist that drifts through Bohemian woods.
Carrying laughter and light
Through valleys, forests, and time.

Praha

Mist curls over the Vltava,
Stones worn smooth by centuries of feet.
The towers rise like quiet sentinels,
And I breathe the hush of history,
Adrift, yet entirely at home.

The Alchemy of Dawn

When I think of Prague, I think of home, but not in the ordinary way one thinks of familiar rooms or comforting places. Prague is a different kind of home, ancient and knowing. It feels older than memory. It feels like a place that recognizes you first. A place that whispers.

At dawn, the Charles Bridge becomes an alchemist.

Night transforms into liquid gold, catching on the cobblestones and trembling in the mist that rises from the river. The city is still half-dreaming, suspended between sleep and waking, and the bridge seems suspended between worlds. It does not yet belong to morning, and it no longer belongs to night.

I step onto the cobblestones, and the stones remember. Their coolness carries the weight of centuries. Footsteps echo beneath my own, layered deep in the mortar: kings and beggars, prophets and lovers, soldiers returning and poets wandering. History does not simply survive here. It breathes.

It rises in the damp air.
It gathers in the crevices of the stone.
It drags like incense above the river.

The saints along the balustrade watch with their patient, timeless faces. Time has softened their edges, but presence has sharpened their gaze. They stand like guardians of untold stories, their silhouettes inked against the dissolving darkness. If you look long enough, if you let the stillness seep into your bones, you almost believe they turn their heads a fraction to acknowledge your walk past them.

The Vltava murmurs like a spell.
Soft. Endless.

A ribbon of flowing history winding through the city's heart. It carries whispers of forgotten courts and vanished rebellions, of lovers who met in secret under the statues, of prayers that drifted into the night long before dawn returned. The river remembers everything. It carries what cannot be spoken anymore and what refuses to be lost.

There is alchemy in this city.

It lives in the way the air tastes, like stone dust mixed with old stones. It lives in the way the street lamps flicker long after sunrise, reluctant to give up their glow. It lives in the way the brick-coloured rooftops the early light and hold it as if it were sacred.

As the sun climbs, the golden haze spills over the city's crown of tiles and towers. Light settles on the cathedral spires and flints on the castle windows with something that feels like a blessing. In that moment, the city feels alive in a way beyond metaphor. Alive as if it has a pulse hidden beneath its cobbled skin.

And with every step I feel my own pulse answer.

Here on this ancient bridge, the morning gathers me gently, as though Prague recognizes me, as though I belong to its story and it belongs to mine.

Seoul

Morning light glints off Han River waters,
Skyscrapers and ancient palaces side by side.
The city hums with lives entwined,
Lanes narrow and fragrant with street food,
And I stand between past and present —
A witness, fully awake, entirely at home.

Pavilions and Shadows

Seoul moves with a pulse all its own. It hums beneath the traffic, beneath the glass towers, beneath the river of people flowing endlessly through streets and subways. Yet, in the midst of this ceaseless motion, there are sanctuaries where the city exhales, where the modern and the ancient meet in quiet intimacy.

Gyeongbokgung stretches before me like a memory folded into the air. The gates shine in deep reds and emeralds, colours shaped by centuries of devotion. Every beam and roof pattern is deliberate, a language of reverence written in wood and paint.

I walk slowly, feeling the centuries press beneath my feet, a tapestry of footsteps — kings, courtiers, soldiers, poets — all whispering into the present. The air tastes of cedar and incense, of earth warmed by sunlight, of the breath of history itself.

By the water, Gyeonghoeru Pavilion floats like a dream suspended in time. Its reflection shimmers across the pond, bending reality with gentle insistence. The water whispers beneath the wooden pillars, carrying with it centuries of laughter, counsel, music, and solitude. Here, the city teaches me patience, stillness, and awe.

Across the river, Bongeunsa Temple waits, a sanctuary in the roar of the modern.

The sound of maemi — cicadas in trance — fills the gardens, their persistent hum is hypnotic. Walking these gardens, my chest loosens. The city's pulse slows to match mine.

I breathe differently here.

Seoul is a city of contrasts. Glass and timber, neon and shadow, past and future, noise and quiet. And yet it holds you in balance.

Every courtyard, every pavilion, every temple teaches something subtle: that beauty is not luxury, that reverence is not a ritual but a lifeline, that history lives not just in books, but in the air you breathe and the stones beneath your feet.

I linger on a bridge overlooking a palace pond. The water shimmers with the reflection of sky waking to dawn, of rooftops layered like folded paper, of trees that have lived longer than I can imagine.

Seoul does not simply exist. It inhabits. It holds. It teaches. It whispers of patience, of wonder, of devotion. And I carry it away with me, not as a visitor, but as a witness, as a heart that has been held by something far larger than itself.

The Language Between

I speak in tongue that twist and bend,
Each word a bridge, each phrase a friend.
Some lips may falter, some hearts may stray,
Yet meaning finds its own way.
The mother tongue, the learned line,
All shape the thought that remains entirely mine.

I move between, I drift, I trace,
The subtle tones that time will place.
Each language holds a world inside,
A way to live, to love, to hide.

The spaces between words carry weight,
Teaching the self to navigate
The quiet currents where meaning waits.

Guardian

I am here, little one,
Your trembling heart safe in my hand.
The shadows that chased you
I will gather and turn to quiet.

Every fear is known,
Every ache is acknowledged.
You may rest here, small and fragile,
And I will stay, unshaken, beside you.

When the night feels endless,
And the world too heavy to bear,
My arms will hold your memory,
Soft as a lullaby,
Until you learn to breathe again.

The Road I Never Took

What if I stepped through another door,
A life untraveled, a distant shore?
The echoes shift, the world turns new,
A different me in skies more blue.

Would love have found me sooner there,
Or drifted past, unseen, unaware?
The paths I never took
Linger like a hush around my heart.

I walk my path, both worn and true,
Yet wonder what I might pursue,
I linger where my footsteps fall,
While unseen roads hum beneath it all.

A Room Within

There is a space that is mine alone –
No doors, no keys, no asking.
The world cannot reach it.

Here, I breathe without shape or name,
Shedding every role I've ever worn.
Here, I am only being –
Unspoken, untethered, enough.

Lingering

I speak in borrowed accents,
My laughter caught between two skies.
At home, my words tumble foreign,
Outside, I twist my tongue to belong.
I am both stranger and translator,
Bearing worlds I cannot set down.

Becoming Ink

I speak in quiet spells across blank pages,
Each letter a step into the life I summon.
Thoughts once trapped behind ribs take shape,
And the world bends slightly to the will of my pen.
I am the maker and the made, the flame and the smoke,
And with every word, I carve a place that is mine.

Ink drips like rain through my veins,
A river I steer towards what I dare to dream.
I call the stories from shadowed corners,
From the edges where the heart trembles.
Becoming ink is becoming myself,
Turning whispers into fire that cannot be silenced.

PART II. Heart Unraveled

The anatomy of love, loss, longing, and heartbreak — the beautiful undoing

He Moves Like Weather

You didn't knock — you moved right through,
Like winds that ancient oaks once knew.
No whispered sign, no warning part —
Just you, and then, a startled heart.

I'd stood untouched by storm or flame,
Then felt you breathe and shift my name.
And now I lean where once I stood,
Not fallen, still here, and bent like boughs,
Deep in the wood, alive beneath the storm.

The Letter’s Weight

I pressed my heart in ink and line,
A fragile script, yet wholly mine.
It crossed the distance, quiet, true –
A paper wind that stirred in you.

You once moved me like sudden skies,
But now my words fall soft, precise.
No random storm, no fleeting call –
Only the quiet that stirred your soul.

Love Letter

She sits at the desk; the room hushed except for the faint hum of evening. Outside, rain taps softly against the window, and the world feels both near and impossibly far. The page before her is blank, yet already heavy with everything she wants to say.

Writing a letter like this is not simple. It is an unspooling of oneself, the careful weaving of admiration, longing, and quiet confession. She writes slowly, measuring each line, aware that the words may never leave this room, may never reach the hands they are intended for, and yet, they demand to be written. There is a tenderness in writing across distance, a surrender to the possibility that someone she has never truly spoken to can still shape her days, her choices, her very being. Each word carries the weight of memory, of quiet observation, of the small ways a person can leave a mark without intending to. She writes of herself, of the life she built, the cities she has walked, the roads that have led her to this evening, the music that has threaded itself through her body and mind like a familiar pulse. She writes of creation, of the small triumphs that go unseen, the work that feels sacred only because it is hers.

There is fear in such intimacy. To place affection and respect on the page is to risk vulnerability, to show the part of oneself that trembles in quiet, unobserved spaces. But she writes anyway, because to withhold would be to deny the truth of what has shaped her heart.

The letter grows longer than she expected. It winds through recollection, hope, and gratitude. It is a map of her own growth, a testimony of what she carries with her. And when she reads it over, there is a quiet satisfaction: this page, this fragment of herself, exists fully, undeniably. It is offered, unadorned, as a gift of presence.

She folds the letter slowly. The rain has softened in mist, the streets glimmering wet with reflected light. The act of writing has done what it was meant to do: it has allowed her to speak without expectation, to witness her own heart, to honour the beauty of connection without claiming it. And in the quiet that follows, she realizes something simple, profound, and certain: to write a love letter is not only to give to another, but to return to oneself.

The Wings I Never Wore

I dreamt, like all, of love's grand flight,
Yet never felt its wings take flight.
A whispered vow, a fleeting spark,
But never dawn – just endless dark.

Hope lingers still, though worn and thin,
A cynic's cage I'm locked within.
Yet love's no chain, nor fate's decree –
Perhaps, it's time to set me free.

Sapphire[3]

Thirteen years, a velvet heart,
His growl a whisper when dreams depart.
Sapphire eyes, soft as dawn's first hue,
Hold the years – and my heart too.

[3] *For Jiji – immortalized in poetry, his velvet heart forever here.*

Unseen Touch

A fleeting shadow,

Hands never touched, lips unclaimed,

Heart waits in silence.

Closed Doors

I spoke my heart, unguarded, unafraid,
For decades built, a fragile bond displayed.
Hope shimmered once where friendship drew its line,
Then vanished, leaving nothing but the fine
Threads of trust, of laughter, of the years,
And all that lingered were the unshed tears.

I step away, yet not in anger's name,
No ghosts of spite, no whispered blame.
I hold the love I felt, fierce, unconfined,
Yet leave the past, the hope, the ties behind.
For self I guard, for peace I must be true –
The door is closed, yet a part of me still holds you.

Like Destiny (운명처럼)[4]

Once a piece of my soul was stolen here. I feel it deep within my heart.

A story stretches across time, and when I first heard your voice, my soul already knew.

We've lived apart in lives before, but fate has opened destiny's door.

Through oceans, years, and endless skies, I find my home where your heart lies.

---

[4] *운명처럼 (unmyeongcheoreom): a Korean phrase meaning "like fate," often used to describe something that feels destined or meant to be.*

Threads of Fate

Once, perhaps, we touched the same flame,
In a life where love had no name.
But stars conspired, the thread was torn,
And so apart, two hearts were born.

Now oceans rise between our hands,
And silence stretches, vast as lands,
Yet every tide, each restless wave,
Reminds me of the bond we made.

If fate demands we toil once more,
To cross the seas, to reach your shore,
Then let the heavens test our will,
For star-crossed hearts are
burning still.

The Song I Never Heard

I wrote the words I could not say,
And tucked them safe, then turned away.
If love was spring, it passed me by,
No blossoms came beneath the sky.
A song half-born, yet left unsung,
A silence where my heart was young.
Two voices near, but never met –
An unplayed hymn, a lost duet.

Yet still I wait, though years grow long,
For silence too can shift to song.
Hope lingers thin, but will not fade,
It threads the dark where dreams are laid.
Perhaps one day the thaw will start,
And love will find my guarded heart.
For though the years have kept me still,
The space remains, the longing will.

Omnia

Tonight, I find myself reflecting on love, that wild, impossible force. Like the one Sappho described in her fragments.

It was always easier not to let myself be seen, to hide from the cruelty that comes when hearts are laid bare. To love fully is to risk being fractured, leaving you to gather the pieces and rebuild yourself, never quite the same.

And yet, here I am. The storm came and I soared, even if only for a moment. My heart was consumed, claimed for another, leaving me to endure the anguish, to burn quietly in silence.

And so, when my wings were torn,

And water doused my fire,

And hollow words silenced my heart's desire,

I let go.

Light[5]

Fifteen years of gentle purrs,
A random heart in softest fur.
You've always been the one I sought,
My childhood wish, my love, my thought.

[5] *For Makgeolli – my ragdoll cat, fifteen years of love and still counting.*

Unfrozen

I stopped believing in love,
Its promises hollow,
Its whispers fading into the wind.
I built walls of careful quiet,
A heart wrapped in shadow and steel.
But you...
You moved through the darkness like light,
And every stone I placed
Shattered under your warmth and might.
I stopped believing in love ...
Until the moment I saw you,
And learned that perhaps it could still be true.

Chrysanthemum

A flower opens in quiet patience
Petals catching the morning light
I feel her there
Her presence folded into the air I breathe.

She watches as I stumble and rise
Tracing the edges of my own heart
Her eyes steady, gentle
Reminding me I am never truly alone.

The scent of chrysanthemums drifts softly
And in it her voice hums
A quiet courage, a tethered love
A promise that I am held
Even when I cannot see her.

I fold my hands over my chest
Learning to honour the fragile, stubborn, luminous self
She has always known I could become.
Petal by petal, breath by breath.

The Echo

The house still keeps your breath.
In the morning, light falls where you once stood,
Dust dancing in its silence.
I do not speak your name
And yet,
It lingers in the air,
Too sacred to disturb.
Love does not die;
It shifts,
Becoming the ache that holds me upright.

Permanence

I swear it to the pulse that keeps me alive,
To the quiet ache that has learned your shape:
My heart remembers you
as the sea remembers the moon,
unmoving in its devotion,
endless in its tide.

Let the years try to erode it,
let absence press its weight against my chest.
This love stands, unyielding, unbroken,
a fire written into the marrow of me.

Wedding Dress

For you, I'd wear a dress made of white,
Woven from the quiet of my longing,
Each fold a pulse of the heart that loves you,
Each seam stitched with the weight of days unspoken.
I would move toward you like sunrise
Spilling light across a darkened room,
Love burning steady, relentless,
Not to claim, but to inhabit the same air as you.
And if the world should bend or falter,
My devotion would hold,
A tide rising and falling,
Eternal as breath, as blood, as this quiet,
Unending vow.

Still

I have loved you in silence –
Through nights that stretched like rivers
And morning that broke without your voice.
For many years, I carried you
As though the air itself could hold you.

I traced your shadow in every doorway,
Learned your laugh in the echo of memory,
And whispered your name
into the hollow spaces of my own chest.
No one knew.
Not a soul.

I have watched you from the edges of my life,
And every step you took,
Every breath,
Was stitched into the fabric of me.
I have grown older, but my heart
Remains a keeper of your light.

If the world bends,

If the stars align,

I will not hide. I will not hesitate.

I will take your hand,

Hold you

As though the years never passed,

And say,

In a voice raw with every stolen second:

I have loved you still –

And I will love you, quietly, always.

PART III. Metamorphosis

The rebirth – of womanhood, power, voice, and resilience

Medusa Rising

They called me curse, a fearsome flame,
A name they twisted into shame.
My hair of serpents, coiled and wild,
A crown, a warning, never child.

I turned my eyes and felt the stone,
The weight of stories not my own.
In silence, though, I claimed my ground,
A quiet strength, no longer bound.

The myths may speak of fear and pain,
But I am more than what remains.
Not monster. Not shadow.
Not broken. Not sold.
I am my fire,
My story,
My gold.

The Quiet Fire

She gives her all, unseen, unheard,
A quiet fire, a whispered world,
Pouring love into the night,
Building worlds without the light.

Her heart beats fierce beneath the strain,
Bearing weight, enduring pain,
Yet in her eyes, a steadfast flame,
Unbroken soul, despite the blame.
She's more than what they understand,
A gentle force, a steady hand.

Though tired, worn, and sometimes torn,
She rises still with every dawn.

To the Self I Lost

I write to you though you cannot reply,
Your voice a whisper, in the empty sky.
The words I send drift through both time and space,
A fragile bridge no hand may ever trace.
I speak of grief, of love of
Paths once crossed,
Of all the things we found and all we lost.

Perhaps I still hope, these words find your eyes,
A glimpse of me beneath these mortal skies.
Though vanished now, your shadows shape my days,
And guides me through life's maze,
I leave these lines where memory may rest.

Wildflower, part II

I do not crave a gilded bed,
Nor walls where roses bow their head.
The wind's my keeper, earth my home,
I flourish most when left to roam.

I fade, I fall, the frost may bite,
But spring recalls my hidden light.
Through death,
Through dark,
I find my way,
And rise anew with each new day.

Inheritance

They say I belong here.
That my voice has built a home on this stage,
That I have a duty – to keep the lights burning
When those hands grow still.
But sometimes,
When the curtain falls
And the applause fades to dust,
I feel another life stirring.
A whisper beneath my ribs,
A heartbeat not yet lived
But waiting, patient,
Like a promise I once made to myself.
I love what was given to me,
But it is not where my heart will bloom.
These roots hold me fast –
And still, I ache to wander.
To start again,
In a place that feels like the first breath after sorrow.

The Storm

I am the daughter of a storm that never learned to rest.
Rooms hum with thunder; words taste of rust.
I sweep up the lightning he leaves behind.
Tired of surviving weather that calls itself love.

Exhaustion blooms in my chest.
I taste the weight pressed there,
 against my ribs,
 the chaos that leaks into every corner.

Yet I remain,
Breathing, aching, alive –
And somewhere inside the wreckage
A different sky begins to form.

The Mortal Self

The body breaks so the soul can speak.

I shed myself like autumn leaves,

Each fall a lesson in beginning again.

To live is to die a thousand soft deaths,

And rise still,

Inked with the memory of them all.

Metamorphosis

I outgrow myself again –

Softly, without apology.

The past unbuttons from my spine,

A garment I no longer need.

What remains is unguarded,

Raw as first light.

There is no audience for this –

Only breath,

And the woman still forming.

The Wildflower I Became

I was not raised in gardens neat,
No guiding hand, no patterned seat.
The winds grew harsh, the soil was thin,
Yet still a bloom took root within.

No walls confined, no fence, no chain –
I learned to blossom through the rain.
Though small, though wild, though oft unseen,
I claimed my place where life had been.

So let the roses fade in line,
Their careful rows will not be mine,
For strength is found where few dare roam –
A wildflower, yet fully home.

PART IV. Palimpsest

The echoes of past lives, history, reincarnation, and spiritual remembrance

The Traveler

I carry no map only memory—

Cities folded in the heart's creases.

Every border I cross blurs the last,

And language becomes a kind prayer.

Dreams Unspooled

I lay my heart beneath the night

Threads of longing spilling into the dark.

Each dream a fragile bird

Fluttering between what was and what might be.

I reach, and shadows stir,

Whispering truths I cannot yet hold.

Where My Heart Remains

I left my heart where old walls breathe,
Through winding alleys, beneath
The curling roofs and whispered pines,
Where shadows dance with ancient lines.

Lantern light spills on cobbled stone,
A quiet hum, a voice not my own.
Footsteps echo, soft and slow,
Carrying memories I can't let go.

A past life lingers in the air,
Soft perfume of blossoms, faint, yet there,
I trace the paths I never tread,
And speak to ghosts I never met.

Evening wind stirs through the gates,
A fleeting vision of what might have been.
Every gate and garden holds my song,
A thousand sunsets in a single eye.

I left my laughter in narrow streets,
My whispered secrets where history meets.
Time folds, yet still I hear the call:
The city cradles a piece of my soul.

So though I wander far and wide,
A shadow of me will always bide,
Among the rooftops, walls, and streams,
In this city of quiet, I keep my dreams.

The Quiet Knowing

In another life, another time, I loved you truly,

No hesitation, no fear –

our hearts were woven together fully.

In this life, though distant, your love still echoes,

The red thread stretches through the ages,

its pull so clear,

though fate has kept us apart,

I know we are destined,

Written in the stars,

And when we meet, we'll soar

as if we've crossed through lifetimes, near and far,

to find each other once more.

And all the waiting,

All the longing,

Will dissolve

Like rain.

Sanctuary[6]

The world unfolds in green and quiet grace,

Temples cradled by the whispering trees.

Below, the city breathes,

a tapestry of stillness and sound.

I stand at the edge, where sky meets memory,

And feel the mountain hold me

Like a prayer.

---

[6] *Inspired by Kiyomizu-dera, the historic hillside temple in Kyoto, Japan.*

Stone Garden

Along the cobble paths, the stones rise

Etched with names, dates, and quiet sighs.

Lichen softens the weight of years,

And sunlight drifts through whispered tears.

Here, history hums beneath the trees,

A gentle pulse carried on the breeze.

In these gardens, I am alone,

Yet never lonely – the past feels like home.

Fractured Mosaics

Beneath the Grecian sun I walked alone,
Where shattered columns claim their silent throne.
Mosaics fractured, yet their colours stay,
A whisper of the lives that passed away.

The temples sigh with echoes of old praise,
Olympia's fields still hold the ancient days.
Once gods and kings were crowned in mortal pride,
Now only dust and wind their secrets hide.

Roots of Belonging

Family is not only what is written in blood
It is the people who sit with you in silence
Who laugh at the same absurdities
Who hear the unspoken and still stay.

It is the hand that reaches for yours
When the world feels heavy
The voice that says
"I see you"
and actually, means it.

I gather these people slowly, carefully
Offering fragments of myself
And receiving their pieces in return.

A tapestry stitched not by genetics
But by trust, tenderness, and time.

In their presence, I am allowed to breathe

To unfold the edges I usually hide

To stumble and be caught

To shine without fear of judgment.

This is a home I build with hearts

Not walls, nor names,

A home of laughter and tears,

Of quiet afternoons and late-night talks

A family I choose,

And they choose me in return

Here, I am whole

Here, I am known.

Old Forest

The air is green with memory,
Petrichor rises from the moss,
As if the earth exhales its dreams.

Roots twist like thoughts too old to name,
And I stand still, listening –
To the slow, deliberate heartbeat
Of something older than time.

Midnight Hall

Cobwebs kiss the walls,

Footsteps echo in the gloom,

Shadows bow to dust.

A Haunting

The house waited for her. Its walls seemed to breathe in the dim light, each floorboard groaning as if remembering footsteps long gone. Shadows clung to the corners, alive with the soft, shifting kind of darkness that made her second-guess the shape of every room.

The air felt thick, scented with damp wood and something older, something that had not breathed for decades. Every creak of the stairs, every soft hiss of wind slipping through a cracked pane, made her heart quicken. She could not tell if the sounds were hers of if the house was trying to speak.

Part of her wanted to run. But something deeper, maybe memory or the strange pull of unfinished stories, kept her moving forward. The hallway narrowed until it reached a door left slightly ajar, a thin slice of darkness waiting on the other side.

She stepped into the room.

Glass glittered on the floor like frost, scrap of burned paper scattered in the dust. A figure hunched near a cold brazier, its form blurred and shifting as though made of smoke or breath. When it slowly turned toward her, the air tightened. The floor beneath her trembled, the shadows stretching long and thin, reaching for her ankles.

For one suspended moment, she felt herself slipping out of time, her pulse syncing with something ancient and wrong. The figure rose, its shape unfurling like a memory trying to stand upright.

She blinked.

The room changed.

No broken glass.

No ash.

No shadows crawling across the floor.

Only sunlight spilling through clear windows, pooling on warm, polished wood.

Whispers in the Wind

The ones I called true turned hollow with ease,
Bending like reeds to a poisonous breeze.
Lies spill like ink, staining my name,
Yet none dare to meet my gaze in the flame.

They dance to the tune of a selfish decree,
Blind to the wreckage, deaf to my plea.
But truth walks steady, unshaken, untamed –
And karma remembers each name.

Venom

I see the sands beneath a burning sky,
A life I lived before, yet cannot die.
A servant girl, her footsteps swift and small,
Fleeing shadows down a temple's hall.

Whispers curl where darkness gathers tight,
A hiss, a coil, a sudden strike of night.
Cold fire spreads unseen, beneath the skin,
And all I was dissolves within.

Lavender, warrior

They asked why I chose a flower
As if softness cannot survive a storm.
But lavender grows through ruin,
Between stones, in silence,
Teaching the air how to heal
What the world has broken.

On my skin, the word warrior breathes,
Not for victories, but for endurance.
I have bled, and still, I bloom.
The petals remember what I've endured,
Their fragrance rising like prayer –
Proof that I am still here,
Still whole, still holy.

Monologue[7]

Do you hear them?

The myths of old? The ones that used to rule these lands and strike the fear of forgotten gods into the faithless crowds? Many consider them a thing of the past, the terrors of a dark age as old as the fallen ruins and yet ... they're still here.

Just listen.

They're in the wind, in the gentle spring breeze that dances above the meandering river. Their secrets hidden in the deep of the calm water and nestled firmly within the crevices of the old ruins above.

---

[7] A monologue written for my father, a gentle nudge from daughter to actor, to draw him back to the stage for my final university project.

Mother

I watch her move through rooms like weather,
Soft rain in the mornings,
A quiet storm by night.
She never says the words that hurt her,
But I see them settle on her shoulders
When she thinks no one is looking.

Her hands smell of flour and dishwater,
Of fixing things no one else notices.
They tuck me in, braid my hair,
Wipe crumbs, wipe tears,
And tremble only when she believes
I am asleep.

Sometimes she sits by the window,
Chin in her palm,
Eyes far away,
As if she is remembering a life

She has not yet lived,

A place where no one raises their voice

And she is not tired.

But there is a glow inside her.

I have seen it,

A small, stubborn ember

She hides behind her smile.

One day I think

That ember will bloom into a sunrise

And she will stand in its light,

Finally warmed by something

That is hers.

And when she does,

I will say nothing,

Just hold her hand

And let her shine.

To walk through memory is to read the pages beneath the pages – each life, each city, each love leaves its mark. The self is written, erased and rewritten, and in those layers, we find the echoes that carry us forward.

PART V. Unbecoming

The letting go – the surrender, peace, and dissolution of the self

Ad Astra

I cast my visions like seeds to the wind,

Bold as fire, relentless as tide.

Each wish a spark, each hope a hymn,

Drawing the world to stand by my side.

I do not wait,

My hands shape the sky,

For dreams well-held will see the day.

Everlight

When I was twelve, the world felt too big,

Its corners sharp, its shadows quick to move.

But you knelt to my height,

Looked me in the eyes,

And the darkness hesitated.

Your hands were small shelters,

Soft places where trembling could rest.

You never asked for bravery from me,

Only breath,

Only one more step forward.

I learned the shape of safety

In the quiet way you spoke my name,

In the warmth of your palm

Guiding me out of the places that scared me.

And now, when fear stirs like an old ghost,
I still feel that moment –
Your steady presence folding the world back
Into something I could bear.

You were the first proof I ever had
That kindness can glow in the dark,
And I carry that glow like a hidden lantern,
Bright enough, even now,
To find my way home.

Magic

It was never in the stars,

Nor in the hands that turned away.

Not in the cities that forgot your name,

Nor in the words that broke you open.

It was always in the pulse you carried,

In the quiet fire behind your eyes,

In the way you stood up –

Again and again,

When the world thought you would fade.

You are the miracle you kept chasing,

The sparkle you thought you'd lost,

You never needed to search for magic.

It was in you all along.

Ourselves

I have learned to sit with myself
As one might with an old friend –
No fixing, no pleading,
Just the quiet warmth of being seen.
I trace my own pulse,
Find rhythm in my breath,
And realize: I am still here,
Still whole, still becoming.

Never Alone

She stands at the window, thirteen, trembling, the world outside too sharp, too loud, too heavy. Every shadow in the room seems to mock her smallness. She turns her face toward the glass as if the glass itself could see her better than anyone else ever did. Behind her, a presence shifts. Older, heavier, carrying scars the girl cannot know yet.

The older self kneels down slowly, carefully, so she does not startle her own past.

“I see you,” she says, voice low but steady. “I have always seen you. I could not protect you then. I was too young, too afraid. But you…you were braver than I ever was.”

The girl flinches, tears gathering like morning dew. “I was alone. They didn’t care. You didn’t see me. You should have stopped it. I wanted someone to stop it. To tell me I mattered.”

The older self swallows the ache in her chest.

"I know. I should have been there. I wasn't. I couldn't. But I can hold it for you now. I can hold the weight you carried so small, so frightened. I can protect you. I will protect you."

A tremor runs through the younger girl. "Do you think...could it have been different?"

"It might have been," the older self admits, voice breaking, "but maybe not. Maybe the piece that broke us built the parts that survived. I would not have been able to hold you now if I hadn't walked through the fire myself. You are enough. You always were enough. And now, I am here. I will not leave you again."

The girl swallows, nodding. The older self can feel the tremor of hope beginning to settle into her bones. "Will I be okay?"

"You will," the older self says, holding her face between her hands. "It will take time, but the fear will loosen. You will learn to breathe in the quiet. You will learn to trust your own strength. And I will be here, always. Even when you forget, I will be here."

Inheritance, Part II

I see the shape of my own name
Etched in places I have yet to go.
I speak, and the voice that answers
Is wholly mine.

What I inherit, I transform.
What I love, I release.
I am not the echo of those before me,
I am the song that begins again.

Unbecoming

I shed the names I never claimed,
The weight of what they called my own.
Each layer falls like autumn rain,
A quiet letting go, alone.
Not all that breaks is lost to night
Some fragments rise, unbound by light.

To let go is not vanish, but to rise – whole, unburdened, and luminous.

Afterword

When I began writing these pieces that would become part of *Unbecoming*, I did not intend to publish it as a book. These were ventures into different places, worlds, observations. I was only trying to make sense of what could not be said aloud – the quiet ache of memory, the ghosts that linger even in joy, the soft insistence of hope that refuses to die.

As the pages grew, I realized something: this wasn't a collection about endings. It was a conversation between versions of myself – the child, the dreamer, the woman, the wanderer. Each writing was a hand reaching out to the next, saying: I see you.

Writing has always been the way I return to myself. It listens when the world does not. It holds space for the moments between heartbreak and healing. It is not a performance. It is prayer. A quiet vow to keep showing up, even when it hurts.

For me, writing feels like freedom. I have the permission to say what I want, as loudly as I want. I can explore anything, share my thoughts, my stories, and perhaps feel confident enough to publish a full-length novel in the future.

As I write this, I am eighteen chapters deep into one mystery-adventure romance novel, and two chapters into another romance-adventure novel. I just want to write, and perhaps publishing this first collection will push me in that direction.

Maybe that is what this whole collection has been – not a linear journey, but a spiral. Every return brings me closer to what I once was, and to what I am still becoming.

If you have read this far, you are now part of that spiral too. You have stepped into the silence I wrote from, and in doing so, you have kept these words alive.

So, thank you.

For listening.

For staying.

For allowing these fragments to meet your own.

Because *Unbecoming* never truly ends. It simply changes shape. And somewhere, beneath all the unraveling, we begin again.

Acknowledgments

To my sister, Martina – the reason this book exists, the fortress who stood when the world pressed too hard. Without you, I would not be here: not in these pages, nor in this life.

To my mother Mária, whose quiet strength has been a constant, steady light. You have taught me resilience, patience and the gentle power of presence.

To my father František, who has shown me the value of perseverance and reminder that courage and curiosity are the keys to living fully.

To my aunt Ann, who has been a steady rock, offering unwavering support and wisdom whenever I needed it.

To all the women in my family – those who have passed and those still present – whose lives, stories and strength have shaped me in ways I cannot fully name.

To my dearest friend Dáša, who is like family and has supported me in all my endeavours – your presence, encouragement, and love have meant the world to me.

To my dearest friend Natasha, my loudest cheerleader, for celebrating every small victory with me and holding space for both my triumphs and frustrations.

To my dearest friend Tsarina, who was the very first friend I made in Canada and who, over the decades, has become like a second sister.

To my theatre family, for your love, unending encouragement, and for becoming more than collaborators – for becoming a family. You have shown me the power of creating, of taking risks, and of holding each other up, on stage and off.

To my Writer Meme Support Group, for the humour, chaos, and midnight motivation that kept the pages turning. You supported me through severe writer's block and cheered me on when I found my flow again. You reminded me that even in the hardest creative moments, laughter and camaraderie can keep a writer moving forward.

To TVXQ, whose music has inspired me since 2006 – for the songs that made me dance, cry, write with my whole heart, and believe in the power of passion, artistry, and love.

To my teachers – past and present – who opened my eyes, pushed me to grow, and showed me that language can be both a mirror and a map. From professors who demanded rigor and precision to mentors who encouraged imagination and boldness, each of you left traces on my writing that will never fade.

To the women writers I admire who wrote before me – Sappho, Shelley, Woolf, Plath, Rice, and all those whose names were lost to history. You whispered across centuries, and I listened. This work would not exist without your defiance and tenderness.

To every friend who read drafts or simply stayed on the other end of a late-night message – thank you for believing that my words mattered, even when I doubted they did.

And to all my readers, including those who had religiously read my fan fictions over the years (that still exist on Archive of Our Own or Fanfiction.net) – your reviews, comments, and hunger for more of my writing have been the fuel that kept me going. Thank you for cheering me on, dreaming alongside me, and showing me that stories can truly connect us across the globe.

This book is built on the love, guidance, and laughter of those who held me when I could not hold myself.

Thank you for being my light, my mirror, and my compass.

ABOUT THE AUTHOR

Natália Vaněčková was born in Považská Bystrica during the final years of Czechoslovakia, growing up with deep roots in both Czech and Slovak heritage. She moved to Canada with her family at age thirteen, carrying with her the languages, stories, and memories of her childhood. A lifelong student of literature, Natália holds a Bachelor's degree in English and has long been inspired by the worlds and voices of poets, novelists, playwrights, and storytellers across time. Early encounters with lyric poetry, especially Sappho's explorations of Eros, shaped her own poetic sensibility, opening a space to write with unflinching intimacy. Though she primarily identifies as a fiction writer, Natália has always embraced poetry, prose, letters, and fragment writing as a form of self-discovery, meditation, and witness to human emotion. *Unbecoming* is her first major collection, a palimpsest of memory, travel, and reflection. Her work draws inspiration from journeys across Asia, Europe, North

Africa, and North and Central America, often exploring memory, ancestry, and the threads connecting past and present selves.

Beyond writing, Natália is deeply engaged in the performing arts. She is a co-founder and one of the directors, and an in-house dramaturge of Naše Divadlo Calgary Ltd., a Czech and Slovak not-for-profit theatre dedicated to sharing Central European stories with Canadian audiences. This work is especially meaningful as Czech amateur theatre is now officially recognized by UNESCO as part of the world's intangible cultural heritage. She is also a singer with the Slovak band SemTam (Here and There) sharing her love of music and language through performance.

Natália lives in Canada, where she continues to write, teach, sing, and explore the world through words, music, and theatre. She is currently developing her first novel, *The Mortal Coil,* a sweeping mystery-adventure set in Central Europe that weaves history, legend, and the human desire to confront mortality.

Moonlight hung low over Prague, casting its pale light like molten silver over the wet cobblestone streets, which shimmered beneath the evening's rain. Shadows draped the Old Town, where ancient spires and domes etched themselves against the night sky. Ahead, Charles Bridge loomed, an imposing figure, its weathered statues of saints silently watching over the city. Below, the Vltava River churned in restless darkness, its waters swallowing the fragmented reflections of the stars.

Footsteps echoed in the silence, quick and uneven, their rhythm frantic against the damp stonework.[8]

[8] *Excerpt from The Mortal Coil by Natália Vaněčková (forthcoming).*

Martin ran. His breath came in ragged gasps, clouding in the sharp winter air. He clutched a small, tightly wrapped bundle beneath his coat, its weight pressing heavily against his chest, far more substantial than its size suggested. His boots struck the cobblestones with desperation, sending up sprays of water from the earlier rain. Each stride took him closer to exhaustion, but the fear gnawing at his heels pushed him onward.[i]

And so the story begins. For now, her voice lives in the quiet, unfolding fragments of *Unbecoming*, but soon readers may follow her into the expansive worlds of her fiction.

---

[i] *Excerpt from The Mortal Coil by Natália Vaněčková (forthcoming).*

www.ingramcontent.com/pod-product-compliance
Lightning Source LLC
LaVergne TN
LVHW051010080826
845145LV00009B/2547

* 9 7 8 1 0 6 7 3 5 2 9 0 5 *